Kids ask

HOW?

HOW do horses sleep?

HOW did people tell time before there were clocks?

HOW can a camel live in the desert?

sequoia™
children's publishing

Illustrated by Marilee Harrald-Pilz

Photography © Shutterstock 2021 mariait; Olga_i; Andrey Burmakin;
Rich Carey; Damsea; ArchMan; Willyam Bradberry; Alexandra Lande; Surachai;
CGi Heart; Dennis Jacobsen; K.A.Willis; Tommy Alven; Skye Studio LK; Gelpi
Photography © iStock ValentynVolkov
Photography by Brian Warling Photography and Siede Preis Photography

Published by Sequoia Children's Publishing,
a division of Phoenix International Publications, Inc.

8501 West Higgins Road   59 Gloucester Place   Heimhuder Straße 81
Chicago, Illinois 60631   London W1U 8JJ   20148 Hamburg

© 2021 Sequoia Publishing & Media, LLC

Customer Service: cs@sequoiakidsbooks.com

www.sequoiakidsbooks.com

ISBN 978-1-64269-349-2

Kids ask

HOW?

Table of Contents

HOW do horses sleep?

Horses usually sleep standing up. Their legs lock in place so they don't fall over. Horses can lie down, but it is hard for them to get back up.

Did you know?

A baby horse can walk when it is two hours old.

HOW big were dinosaurs?

There were hundreds of types of dinosaurs. They came in all sizes. The smallest dinosaur was the size of a chicken. Other types were bigger than a school bus.

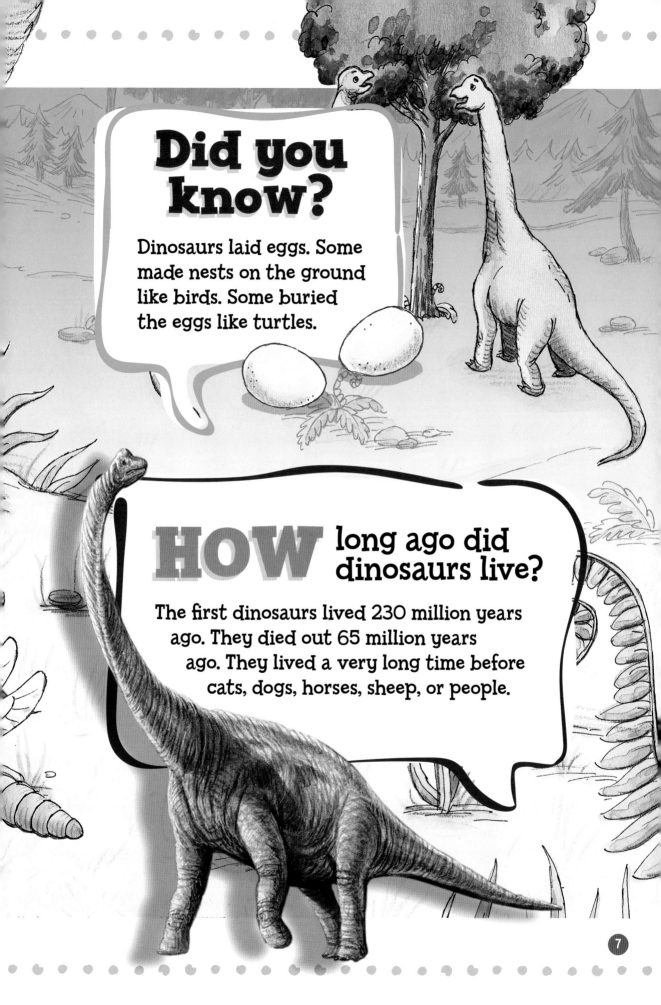

Did you know?

Dinosaurs laid eggs. Some made nests on the ground like birds. Some buried the eggs like turtles.

HOW long ago did dinosaurs live?

The first dinosaurs lived 230 million years ago. They died out 65 million years ago. They lived a very long time before cats, dogs, horses, sheep, or people.

HOW did people tell time before there were clocks?

Before clocks, the sun helped people tell time. The sun moves across the sky each day. That changes how shadows look. People can look at shadows to tell the time.

Did you know?

Before clocks, people could use an hourglass to keep track of time. An hourglass has sand in it. It takes one hour for the sand to flow from one end to the other.

HOW do fish breathe underwater?

Fish use gills to breathe. Gills are like lungs! They help fish get oxygen from the water. People get oxygen from the air.

Did you know?

Whales and dolphins look like fish, but they are mammals. They have lungs, like us. They have to stick their heads out of the water to breathe.

HOW deep is the ocean?

In some places, the ocean is seven miles deep. That is deeper than the tallest mountain in the world! The water down there is very cold and very dark.

HOW can a camel live in the desert?

Camels drink a lot of water when they can. Then they store the water in their body. They have wide, thick feet. This helps them walk on hot sand.

Did you know?

The spitting cobra can shoot venom out of its teeth. The venom can go eight feet!

HOW does a snake move without legs?

Snakes have many little bones along their back. Their muscles move and bend the bones. This moves their bodies forward.

HOW does an airplane fly?

An airplane has wings that are a special shape. When the plane goes fast enough, the wings move the air around the plane in a certain way. The air gets the plane to go up.

Did you know?

A sheep, a duck, and a chicken were the first hot air balloon passengers.

HOW do people steer a hot air balloon?

You can't steer a hot air balloon. You can only make the balloon go up or down. The wind moves the hot air balloon around. To fly a hot air balloon you have to know a lot about wind.

HOW high can a kangaroo jump?

A kangaroo has very strong legs and a strong tail. It can jump as high as a basketball hoop. If it is hopping as fast as it can, it can jump the length of a school bus!

Did you know?

A baby kangaroo stays in its mother's pouch until it is more than a year old.

HOW does a roller coaster stay on the track?

Roller coasters have three sets of wheels. One set is on top of the track. One set is on the side of the track. One set is on the bottom of the track. The wheels make sure the roller coaster stays on the track.

Did you know?

Some roller coasters go over 120 miles per hour. That is almost two times faster than a car on the highway.

HOW much can people learn?

The brain is amazing. It can take in all kinds of information. It can store more than any computer! People can learn just about anything they want to learn.